DR. MURIEL MCCLELLAN

ADVICE FROM THE Grizzly Bears

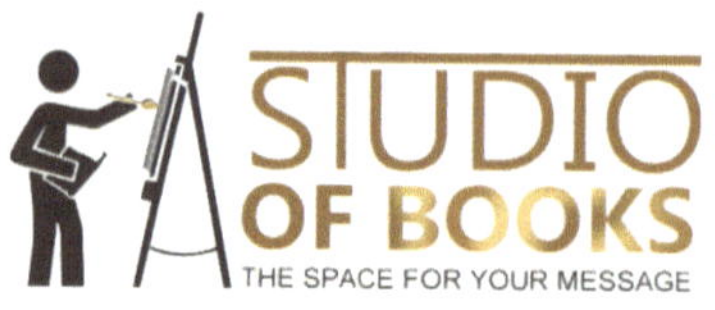

Studio of Books LLC
5900 Balcones Drive Suite 100
Austin, Texas 78731
www.studioofbooks.org
Hotline: (254) 800-1183

Ordering Information:
Special discounts are available on quantity purchases by corporations, associations, and others. For details, contact the publisher at the address above.

Printed in the United States of America.

ISBN-13: Softcover 978-1-968491-74-1
eBook 978-1-968491-75-8

Library of Congress Control Number:

In Advice from the Grizzly Bears, Dr. Muriel McClellan blends together her knowledge as a psychologist with her love of wildlife photography. After completing her Ph.D. in Counseling Psychology from Arizona State University, she went on to establish a successful counseling practice. Yet, she was drawn to nature and eventually took up wildlife photography. Dr. McClellan went to Africa to photograph elephants and lions; Japan to photograph red crowned cranes and snow monkeys; England to photograph puffins; Greece to photograph Dalmatian pelicans; the Antarctica to photograph penguins; and recently to Lake Clark National Park and Preserve in Alaska to photograph brown bears ... know as grizzlies.

It was through her travels in Alaska that she began to envision a book telling the story of bears speaking to her and asking that she share their wisdom. The book would be full of photos capturing the beauty of Alaska and bears in the wild. Each photo would have a caption combining her knowledge of psychology with ideas from the bears that could be applied to one's daily life. Advice from the Grizzly Bears is a result of that vision.

This book can be used in many ways and is thought provoking to adults, as well as children. One can read it alone to reflect on certain ideas. It can be read to children as a way to encourage them to think about choices they can make. Therapist can use the book in counseling sessions to break the ice, especially with young children or teenagers who might not open up easily.

Dr. McClellan hopes that you will enjoy these delightful photos and that the captions will help you live a more satisfied life.

Look your best when someone is taking your picture.

You never know where it will be posted on social media.

Rest once in awhile and hangout in nature.

After you are rested, hop to it and get something done.

Bears need trees to scratch their backs ... so save the forests.

Clean water is very important ... don’t pollute our streams.

This is not the way to solve your problems ...

it would be better to put your feelings into words and negotiate a win-win solution.

Being still and quiet is good
for the soul.

But sometimes you just have to get somewhere quickly.

It is not very nice to stickout your tongue.
Be honest and don't just claim you were only yawning.

Please learn to chew with your mouth closed.
You might also consider using a napkin.

Consider using your foot to scratch under your arm.
Anything is possible out of necessity.

Even though you would like to sleep in, when it is time to get up, get up!

Take time out to reflect on your future
and consider your options.

Exercise is very important.
Sign up for a “yoga bear” class o
water aerobics.

Don’t just cross your legs for luck and wait.
It is better to take action.

Make the world a better place.
Raise your hand and volunteer.

If you know someone who gets terrible headaches,
give them sympathy ... but don't give them the headache.

Don’t be a drama queen just to try and get your way.

Food and water are very important.

Consider being a vegan and enjoy a plant based diet ... until the salmon runs.

Sometimes you just have to hang on and get support.

If you are sad or depressed, talk to someone.
Do not hurt yourself ... this too shall pass.

Elections are important.
Stand up and be counted.

The Pledge of Allegiance ends with “and justice for all.”
That means brown bears, black bears, and gummy bears.

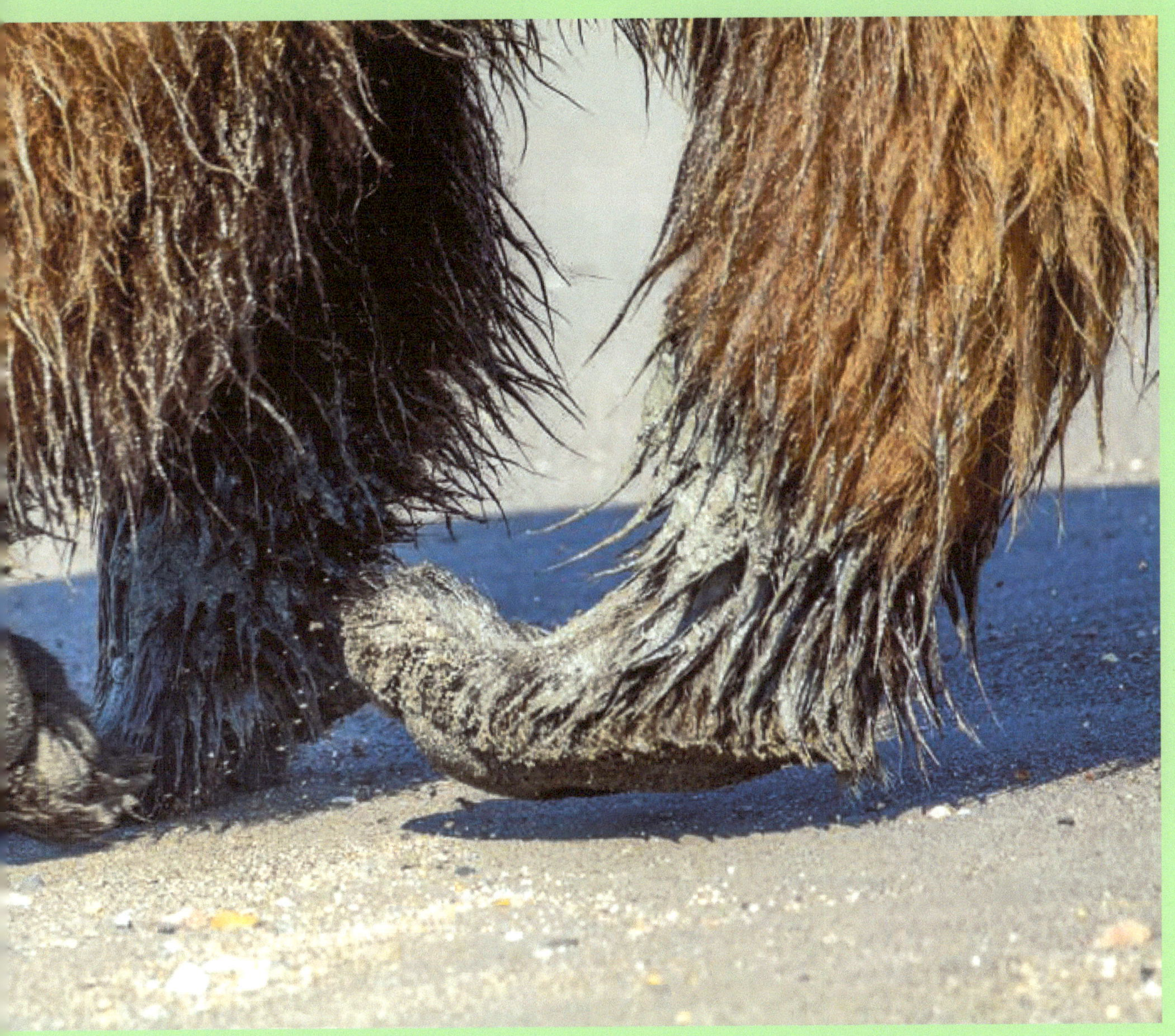

Probably not a good idea to come into the house until you wash your feet.

Show your strength by the ability to have respect for others.

In other words, be the bigger person.

Not every one is good looking. A kind heart might be better than good looks.

If you see something that bothers you, don't just sit there and watch.

Speak up ... even if you have food in your mouth.

A comfortable pillow can help with a good nap.

Try a mindful meditation, it is better than abusing drugs.

Be like a Grizzly Bear and spend time in nature ...
a great place to meditate.

But most of all, stop and smell the flowers.

www.ingramcontent.com/pod-product-compliance
Ingram Content Group UK Ltd.
Pitfield, Milton Keynes, MK11 3LW, UK
UKHW060101300726

14090UKWH00003B/341

9781968491741